On the Poems in *The Listener Aspires to the Condition of Music*

"I know of no other selected poems that selects on one theme, but this one does, charting Goldensohn's career-long attraction to music's performance, consolations and its august, thrilling, scary and clownish charms. Does all art aspire to the condition of music as Pater claimed, exhaling in a swoon toward that one class act? Goldensohn is more aware than the late 19th century of the overtones of such breathing: his poems thoroughly round out those overtones in a poet's lifetime of listening."
John Peck, poet, editor, Fellow of the American Academy of Rome.

"Barry Goldensohn has long been a poet of many measures: now intricate and allusive, now tender or severe, here ecstatic, there playful and colloquial. But again and again in his work he has allowed music to lead him to the deepest places, where contraries are evoked and accommodated as they have been only very rarely in our poetry. His newest volume, devoted entirely to the subject of music, brings us poems sovereign and whimsical: the pianist with "gunfighter's hands," the music of love and the loss of love, the strains of a music powerful enough to 'rouse to sexual frenzy the eroded statues of the female saints.' With this new book, drawn from the work of a lifetime, Goldensohn reminds us why he has long seemed to many of us ever fresh and sustaining."
Robert Boyers, editor, *Salmagundi*

"These music poems quietly accumulate our desperate need for art."
Paul Nelson, poet, former Director of Graduate Program in Creative Writing at Ohio University

The Listener Aspires
to the Condition of Music

Poems
Barry Goldensohn

Art
Douglas Kinsey

Fomite
Burlington, Vermont

Poems Copyright © by Barry Goldensohn
Art Copyright © by Douglas Kinsey

All rights reserved. No part of this book may be reproduced in any form or by any means without the prior written consent of the publisher, except in the case of brief quotations used in reviews and certain other noncommercial uses permitted by copyright law.

ISBN-13:   978-1-937677-10-7
Library of Congress Control Number: 2011939153

20120628
Fomite
58 Peru Street
Burlington, VT 05401
www.fomitepress.com

Cover Art - Douglas Kinsey

All arts constantly aspire towards the condition of music.

Walter Pater, *The Renaissance*

ACKNOWLEDGMENTS

The Listener Aspires to the Condition of Music, *St. Venus Eve*
Padre Antonio Vivaldi, *St. Venus Eve*
Don Giovanni: Last Act, *Salmagundi* and *The Marrano*
Dichterliebe, *AGNI*
Time and the String Quartet Domesticate Eros, *Poetry* and
    Uncarving the Block
Lute and Virginal Outdoors, *Southern Poetry Review*
String Quartet, *The New Republic*
Thelonious Monk Dancing, *Harvard Review*
Rest, *Salmagundi*
The Religion of Art, *Salmagundi*
Marching Band, *Uncarving the Block*
What *is* the Condition of Music?, *Our Generation* (Montreal) and
    Uncarving the Block
Before Beethoven's Creation of Music as Personal Expression,
    Poetry and *The Marrano*
Burmese Temple Bell, *Uncarving the Block*

BOOKS BY THE SAME AUTHOR

Saint Venus Eve, 1972
Uncarving the Block, 1978
The Marrano, 1988
Dance Music, 1992
East Long Pond (with Lorrie Goldensohn), 1998

Table of Contents

The Listener Aspires to the Condition of Music 3
The String Quartet 4
Time and the String Quartet Domesticate Eros 6
Padre Antonio Vivaldi 8
What *Is* the Condition of Music? 9
The Religion of Art: 1 Feb 58 11
Last Act: *Don Giovanni* 13
Lulu (after Alban Berg) 15
Carmens, The Audition 16
Before Beethoven's Creation of Music as Personal Expression . 17
Performance 18
Lost Yellow Dress 19
Thelonius Monk Dancing 20
Funeral Beginning with Bach 22
Gesualdo in Concert 23
Dichterliebe, For Voice and Piano 24
Desire 26
Late Quartet 29
Marching Band 30
Lute and Virginal Outdoors 32
Hearing Schubert's Cello Quintet Again 35
The Harmonium 36
Choral Concert, St. Pancras Old Church 37
David and Saul 38
Burmese Temple Bell 39
The Bells 40
Rest 42
About the Artist 45

The Listener Aspires to the Condition of Music
    for Janos Starker's performance of the Bach cello suites

Because a bow across a cello
moves with such precision that the strings
fill the air with that progression of exact
vibrations that ensnare the air, that hammer,
anvil, stirrup all transmit the movement
of, and move themselves, and move
the mind in such complex voluptuous
sensations, moving everything within to make
it dance its court and country dances in a
suite of dances no human body
ever danced or could dance in many voices
that sing out from each stroked string,
something in us dances, lets us die
a little, making music of us, of the still
gross grounded lump that listens.

THE STRING QUARTET

The first violinist, all of him, follows his arm,
his feet sway around him to keep him in
balance as he sways and lunges into the sounds he makes.
This is dance making music of the body.

The face of the second violinist is Unending Passion.
Such expressiveness, such deep response, would rouse
to sexual frenzy the eroded statues of the female saints.
His is the face of music as romance.

The cellist grinds his teeth, clenches his face in spasms
of control to keep down the groan, the song, the wild
lament he lets his bow alone sound across the strings.
His is the grimace of dignified loss in the tragic agon.

The violist sits and plays. Staid. In his face
the years in Brussels, tutelage at the old Conservatoire
grubbing for meals, going back for practice, practice.
This is music itself as it leaves the body behind.

Time and the String Quartet Domesticate Eros

They are tempestuous in white ties,
black suits and gleaming shoes, seated.

And what proceeds from them in C
sharp minor surely is tempestuous.

It subverts all other order. Abandon
is delicious and to such

ecstatic stuff! It was arranged
to end. We turn, stand, bang

our knees against the seats, fumble
with our coats, remind ourselves

of home, return. We never once
dreamed of real submission.

Padre Antonio Vivaldi

Every day, even on the dog days,
the fat Padre plays the harpsichord
in the stucco courtyard. Children dance
around him, race around that elegant
inlaid instrument, around the lush trees
whose broad leaves are nearly black. The yard,
the high walls, are lurid—yellow as lemons.
When Padre jumps up, runs, they never know
whether he will join them in their ring
that stress of brilliant energy sustained
or pirouette florid and screaming.

WHAT *IS* THE CONDITION OF MUSIC?

Music as Civic Order

Ringing the tables of the gaudy plaza
with heads together they buzz and they sway over
scores like forsythia in a strong wind.
Waving their arms and their hands
conducting the shapes out of air,
they weave in their frail steel chairs.
                              Busy.
They will never offend *il Principe*; easy
to govern. The Mayor is lazy, the sheriff
rocks his bulk back in his chair,
his raised feet dance in the air,
a coda, a musical close.

Outlaw Music

Well, now that's over, the door
burst in, the wall split through which
the heavy breathers push to fill
the tight house with dancing, drowning
in the deaf-making music and belching
from the beer that still burbles
from the stone prick of Dionysus
and the girls forget themselves, skirts
above their breasts as they flash their white
unsunned asses and the house is all meat,
shrieks and hair, bracing body salts
and ecstasy with everything thrown back,
walls and heads, mouths and all throats
pouring full and lost in all that opening.

THE RELIGION OF ART: 1 FEB 58

No one more remote than us
at twenty. I seem doll small
in memory: the lens long focus—
a tiny man, a tiny hospital.

For a full day we timed contractions,
you dozed, I read aloud to you
how son kills father, father son,
in *Don Juan* by Victor Hugo.

The Don, while canonized at Mass,
wrings off his head in his high coffin,
flings it and kills the spiteful priest.
Better a devil of liberation

than be a saint. You were being natural
until delivery and gas.
It was a simple country hospital,
no nursery, no wall of glass.

I got to see you, stunned face
to face with Matthew in your arms.
You were so addled with the nurse
you forgot my name for the state forms.

When I left you on your high bed
you were white—a porcelain flask.
Our new son was bright red
and puckered like a dragon mask.

I too was dazed, so mastered by what
I thought I should feel, I never knew
what I felt—desperate
to kneel, to celebrate with you.

But I could never really force my breath
to thank for this single time he skipped
us, the child killing Angel of Death
who delivered us bathed in blood from Egypt.

It's what I thought was due, to buy
my son from death. I had the rite wrong.
I only had to claim him from the rabbi
(who never had him) for a song.

A tiny refusal. Your time was full.
My mind stank with the need for prayer.
In the religion of the Great Dispersal
my shul was the record player

turning the world on auto-repeat
eight times, before I could find
the firmness of Bach's first Cello Suite—
how adequate that sculpting of my mind.

LAST ACT: *DON GIOVANNI*

He understood no other name but death
for the wish to be restrained, and the Stone Guest
invited in defiance clomped across the room
and the massed silver clattered on the table
at each footfall, the last feast
to end the comic murderous lust and send
Giovanni and his phallus errant
cursing through the trap door and stage flames.

He had no inner life—no check and counter—
an animal attack against the law
without love, with one drive only,
to push into the soft door, either
open in passion or closed and dry in terror.
He was a numbers man: a finite
linear series that comprehends its end.

In this extremity, let us offer unction.

For his eyes whose rolling hunger we have guessed,
let them (Amen) close and ears that heard
much squealing in the highest register
of acquiescence, though protest was music too,
hear, after your applause, nothing more (Amen).
It is said he missed much loamy richness
because he kept his nose stopped with wax
though this is an addition to the text

by the too fastidious which he was not.
Let it now be stopped (Amen). His mouth,
the taste of other mouths, and his lies—
how sweet on the tongue they were—how much
like civilized duplicity—on their account
forebear and wish that mouth its dry peace (Amen).
The hands that alone or with others gave
much pleasure, and received, and agony,
let their bones brown richly among their rings
forever undisturbed (Amen) and feet
that pointed downward for release rest now
not splayed, relaxed, but propped (Amen) upright.
And for the instrument whose instrument he was,
let it decline into perpetual rest, the terror
he dreamed of. He was his own instrument.

Lulu (after Alban Berg)

Leering, leaning over my chair,
he was a bear, uncombed, half-dressed,
speaking too loud, too close:
"I'll show you the real beast,"
waving at her, his intimate terror.

Her body like a leopard. He followed
like a leopard, noting her guard
to catch it down at a soft moment
or defend her as his own, hard
his teeth against her teeth, sweet blood.

Locked in this. To be envied,
the courage of desire swollen so great
tolling through him as he followed
the strong musk, the weight
of sumptuous hair she brushed aside,

the falling and the loose. As she listened
in her low gown she spread
her body into a moist knowing smile
that grew across the vast bed,
heated the room, and glistened.

CARMENS, THE AUDITION
    Jamais Carmen ne cédera!
    Libre elle est née et libre elle mourra!

Enter two ill matched women
casting for Carmen—the law of their beauty
occludes the safety codes
designed to protect and torment.
One is soft-featured, soft-bodied,
blonde, unpracticed, yielding,
a fine singer spoiled by her gift,
the Carmen you forgive everything,
a victim of her power she fails
to understand: innocent
arrogance, instinctive freedom,
the wound that invites the knife.
We weep for her. The other
a studio tan brunette, focused
lean face, tight mouth,
eyes that master the whole room,
knows her desires and gets them met.
Freedom requires power and she grasps it
but doesn't. *Carmen will never yield.*
She was born free, she will die
free, boasts Carmen of herselves,
who dream that they choose,
but do not expect to die
ever, nor understand their enemy:
its possession thwarted,
love murders.

BEFORE BEETHOVEN'S CREATION OF MUSIC AS PERSONAL EXPRESSION
—a vigil for Lorrie

At her bedside all day and she unconscious—
tubes in, tubes out, tape and bruises,
clamps, catheters to the heart, some thing
breathing for her, monitors murmuring, knowing
that nothing was yet out of control of the doctors.

And then home and music and collapse
and Beethoven's Quartet in G,
very classical, impersonal,
before his revolution made everything
Beethoven! Beethoven! and my outstretched nerves
the strings they played sweet repetitive
symmetrical structures on—clear, small surprises
that carried me far from myself into myself.

Nothing was yet out of control of the doctors,
the team, their exquisite machines for reading the heart,
breathing for her, monitors murmuring, knowing
this is a vigil I did not keep for my mother,
years ago, she also unconscious,
and neither woman knew whether I kept it or not.

PERFORMANCE
        for Richard Goode

He is the emblem of rapture, singing to himself,
wordless, soundless, making faces
like Chinese dragons, all of himself
is in the singing, soulfully, wholly,

and the piano seems merely a prop in this other performance
as his hands and fingers just follow along with the song
and the music we hear comes bouncing along
away from the sounding board open wide

on the big voiced instrument in formal concert black
that looks like it wants to leap out of his hands
and charge off on its own, but stays
and plays the song he sings to master it.

LOST YELLOW DRESS

I woke up this morning with a song banging round my head,
Bessie Smith singing with vibrating throbs and wails
about her lost yellow dress, how she loves that yellow dress,
trimmed with blood red and black and all she could do,
with the whole world's sorrow in her voice
and its knowledge that assaults and assails
because she knows she won't get that yellow dress back.

THELONIUS MONK DANCING

What might this figure of great force do?
Or not do? Seeming uncontrolled he hit
and poked at the piano without error
then rose and wandered off around the floor

doing a march time heavy footed non-dance
dance, slow turns, clown twirls, arm flaps, he cowed
us, massive, dazed and full of drunk
menace and disdain for the college crowd

at the Five Spot. His deep control relaxed
and grew perilous, crazy, a wounded bear
mugging at the dates of pretty girls. I
was confused and frightened for him and for

myself—what humiliation would I be called
to witness or undergo, what fall or fight,
with this genius drinking himself to greater
distance, building distraction or rage—how could

any of us tell? The waiters kept his whiskey glass
on the piano filled, fuelling the veering
circuit that ignored then threatened
then disdained to destroy us out of love

for something more important than ourselves.
Helpless, polite, white, we disappeared
behind his music, then Ray Copeland's singing
horn brought him round and the drums calmed him

and recalled him to play the piece that had run
through so many variations on the vibes,
sax, horn and drums that only one who could take
a phrase in four directions at once could make it end

as music. He steered his mocking shuffle back to the piano
and his feet danced and his fast gunfighter's hands
on the keys, played and not played, turned the room—
terrorized, confused—into his rich, perilous music.

Funeral Beginning with Bach

Not another bumbling folksong dressed
in concert black and white, but the austere
tempered formal exercise that turns
through the permutations, all possible
fugues, caring nothing for the language
of the throat burning with the heart's acid,
or the acid heart itself, spewing itself.
It is the time for pure sound itself,
simply in order, order itself in order.

But after music tempers the breath
and drives the body to throb and shake,
according to its firm domination
and drenches the mind,
                                language stumbles in,
with pants around his knees, shirt twisted,
shaking, unaware of the trouble he makes
as he fumbles to straighten his feet
with a too elaborate deliberation
(—*Is he drunk?—He looks drunk.*)
yet he cannot ever stop trying
to disentangle himself from his own deceit
to tell us the story we really need to know,
lying his way into greater confusion.
(—*Look at that convoluted brain!*)

GESUALDO IN CONCERT

In a Protestant church in Paris, bare walls,
large wooden cross without Christ,
a lectern for pulpit, ornate Gesualdo
erotic and liturgical madrigals
reverb off these walls in his unique
archaic and invented modes, so outlandish
no composer dared to use them again
for three hundred years. They weren't singing
just the vowels. With him one sings
the whole passionate word. For his Protestant hosts
he is the exemplary Catholic: intricate mind,
highly wrought ecstatic music,
a multiple murderer (his wife, her lover,
Duke of Andria, and suspected of others),
a sadist and devoted masochist,
a compact of sins. The audience agog,
a girl at my side hardly breathing
to create a silence that makes way for the music
and she is staring with her whole face,
eyes and mouth agape, nostrils flaring,
to see, to taste, to smell the music,
and here, histories of bloody enmity—
Catholic and Protestant, Hindu,
Moslem, Jew, are transfixed by discordant
harmonies and stunned to a fleeting truce.

DICHTERLIEBE, FOR VOICE AND PIANO

Before the notes of the piano, all
exact, well-tempered, many-voiced and pure,
so precise in pitch and time and phrase,
so many that they climb the scales or fall
in chords, retard, advance and order
each note's attack and fade with such control
that when the voice enters, groping about,
searching for notes, laboring, huffing its words,
swells to reach, rises then sinks again
to its own note and always the piano,
clear, as the coarse voice modulates
against it, croons, grunts and roars (with pauses
and wavers that show the singer thinks his life
and feelings matter to us, should matter)
as it stumbles like a dancing bear before
a dulcimer and flute in a gypsy's hands
and lumbers off balance in rancid fur
and pants out its garbage eating breath,
stands in its yellow hat and bulging pants,
then lifts one heavy foot and lets it fall,
then lifts the other, and faster, and dances Bear—
and bears at last this trying-to-say-with-words—
transfixing that it means or moves at all.

DESIRE
> *in the Salle Cortot*

The rapt concentration on their faces
as they focus on their violins, viola,
makes them beautiful, these aged men
who circle the young cellist, her vaulting brow,
full mouth with its tense French poise
and large eyes that roll with the music
with her strong thighs wrapped around the enviable cello—
they must all love her—I love her—
they with their fusion of carefully modulated passion,
calculation and precise action of mountaineers,
radiant with intense devotion
to the game with pitch and time—rhythms
of dubious, irresponsible languor or passion
or the delight in pattern, the music of the movement
of mind that leads and orders the struggle for words,
the dance, the rhythms of desire, the great fugue.

LATE QUARTET

The second violin is a beautiful woman, Korean,
in a skin tight black dress, whose flexible
body expresses every note she plays
but the real action, alas, is in the square
suit named Pigeon, the first violin.
The passion that pours from him leaves
him looking unmoved, untouched. His thin
face is pinched into a dead smile while she heaves
and lunges through her dull repeats, repeats.
How contained this musical storm is, in its little crock.
This crock contains, however, seven oceans
and all the continents except ice-locked
Antarctica, with its penguins, its taciturn orca,
its groaning ice, all deplorably unmusical.

Marching Band

A band, high brass, a faint relentless beat
dividing into random counterpoint
around the Civil War Monument,
approaching, and increasingly distinct,
a full procession chanting, and your office mate
stares at you, turns away, lights a cigarette
and down the straight avenue the band's
sound increases, the crowd runs in advance;
chattering and eyes and the low window;
you deny no longer that you know; the chant
is peaceful this close; a drummer in a campaign hat
wanders away tapping idly; you can
no longer resist moving out into the street
to be in a firmer position to hear the news
they have come to deliver formally: defeat
of your main force, loss of the world and desire,
the cement abrades your knees, you feel it
against your teeth, they lift you as you fall
trying to escape the last words of that choir.

LUTE AND VIRGINAL OUTDOORS

With the fervor of lovers they hunch over
their small voiced instruments
and caress a sound from them the wind
that sighs across the lake
blows as it lists our way or away.
All manic and minute attention
she embraces her lute with bare arms
surprisingly delicate and thin
emerging from her puffed half sleeves
but they move within their small scope
with great deliberation. His shoulders
and his hands are hunched over the tiny
wooden keyboard of his virginal
that lies overwhelmed
beneath the dome of his large frame.
We should be close packed to hear
what they hear, the order that they make for us,
we should toddle in, fearless,
head to his chest, head on her lap.

HEARING SCHUBERT'S CELLO QUINTET AGAIN

The speed of flow of my blood, the firing
of every nerve, the familiar motions of my body,
deathly slow, defying my heart to stop, or racing
as the mind can race from the low tones
of the two cellos to the top notes of the violins
played on the strings of my nerves themselves
and my body and mind are the music itself,
the bows and instruments, the arms,
hands, fingers, minds containing music,
five voices, when they enter and the sounds
they make, possessed, as an infant at the breast,
gorged on a nipple, then lifted and carried
pressed close, everything surprising,
unpredictable, everything in place,
and set down where I knew I should be.

The Harmonium

The music of the poor parish and outposts of the faith
among the remoter pagans to unbenight with hymns,
their foot powered bellows rendered archaic
by the Hammond organ, the remaining harmoniums
rot in rural barns. A friend bought one to revive
its ancient virtues: patched up, varnished,
tuned again, he played the Anglican hymns,
and some dances Bach wrote for his wife
Anna Magdalena's harpsichord
that the harmonium muddied on its gasping reeds.
My friend was no collector of antiquities,
he was just sentimental about his past
and the lost past, the unquestioning glories
of his father's and grandfather's day,
their privilege, their strenuous faith,
and strove to lure them back with music,
the musty smell of it, the sharp taste
of that world they strode through in command.

CHORAL CONCERT, St. Pancras Old Church

Against the terror of cessation
of the mind's play, of eye, tongue
tasting and talking, ear, nose, skin,
and the advent of absolute nothing
those in the hope of life eternal built
church on crumbled church on this same ground
that venerates a boy of fourteen
beheaded for Christ in 303 and made
a saint to pray to for relief from cramps,

where we come to hear the true enduring structures,
polyphony in graduated voices, singing
kyrie, gloria, credo, bits of liturgy
transcending the rote pieties that invoke
dead answers to our cries and questions.

David and Saul

Observed, discreetly, by members of the court
when David sings, Saul grasps his spear.
The pundits blame Saul's madness,
but others, outside the court, say it's power—
the god-talk and the liberating tunes
of David as he sings enrage Saul.
His flagrant dazzle, rapture and spells
trivialize the authority of kings.
Saul gnashes his teeth, knots his face.
Think of poor Stalin, unable to kill
lucky Shostakovich. If not for the music,
if it were just poems, he could kill.

BURMESE TEMPLE BELL

Each dawn this great bell
is struck for each sin
one hundred eight blows:
the world is gathered in
the circle of its voice
and everywhere within
a great order rung.
It tolls through the school
where sleepy children learn
the ciphers and the rule
to wear inside the face
not rule but sub-rule
that they can never break.
They chant in unison,
breathe in its metal breath,
their cheeks to its brass skin.
My own careless life
summoned by this bell
with its low resonance,
from dreaming half awake
or dawdling with words in a room,
would lose the small self,
the small waste of time
in that trembling embrace and dance
that calls me whole to home.

The Bells

Across the street the busy church and school
broadcasts its bells every fifteen minutes
not a decent hourly interval, or real bells.
They do not call my friends who are lapsed Jews
to prayer, to class, to any common life
in this community of which they are no part.
It is like the unattended chatter from which politeness
cannot escape. No sinister communion
threatens by this noise, no betrayal
of their buoyant skeptical faith, no protection
from werewolf or vampire or car bomb.
Across the street the folks in uniform,
priests and students, scurry between assignments,
when the young are not tumbling garbage cans,
breaking windows, slashing tires, spraying
their names on walls and other ceremonial acts.

Rest

There were real ducks in the pond arched
by willows and even the Quakers
tolerated music in the service
(it seemed like pure lament and not
a brash display to false gods)
and I suffered an intense nostalgia
for the self deceiving dream order,
promises, prayers, gifts, bribes,
and all flesh will come to thee,
and all come home and home-free-all
as we gathered in the light around
the casket of this slight young
woman--beautiful even dead.
Her hair combed straight, she always
seemed a veiled Botticelli,
now with eyelids strictly closed.
From the sexual center cancer everywhere
closed her lungs and she lay very still
in the last days and tried to live
without breathing. Now her real
body remains with a cross in her hands
that beckons upward to the grand design.
And they sang Mozart's *Requiem* that begins
and ends with a prayer for *them,* the dead,
who need eternal rest, perpetual light,
the soul that pleads in terror for mercy
from the judgment at the world's end

that frightens even the just and the virgins.
Salva me, fons pietatis,
fountain of pity, save me.
We learned enough of dread in hope,
even thinking she beat it, that vital
body beat it. There was comfort
in remission for weeks that seemed
perpetual light. Now the cry
of terror takes on ritual fullness,
Salva me...non me perdas...
with music we wished her eternal rest
in the arms of her torturer and killer.
And for our grieving all these voices
in the large musical structure sufficed:
it wasn't overwrought, and the prayer,
not abject, loose talk
about the soul. For all the show
of theatrical emotion, there
was dignity and no shame
in this fear. It is the way, lost,
we want ourselves spoken of, sung of.

About the Artist

Douglas Kinsey is a painter and monotyper. He has exhibited throughout this country as well as in England, Sweden and Japan. His illustrations have mostly been for books of poetry. For twelve years he has been a Professor Emeritus at the University of Notre Dame, but early on he taught in the University of North Dakota as well as in the colleges of Berea and Oberlin. He is also a musician who plays early music.

The monotypes in this book were developed from a shiny zinc plate which was first rolled with black ink. Some of the dark was then wiped with a cloth, revealing surface and the light. The image was further clarified by the use of brush and ink as well using the other end of the brush to uncover white lines. The images were printed in an etching press.

Fomite
Burlington, Vermont

Fomite is a literary press whose authors and artists explore the human condition -- political, cultural, personal and historical -- in poetry and prose.

A fomite is a medium capable of transmitting infectious organisms from one individual to another.

"The activity of art is based on the capacity of people to be infected by the feelings of others." Tolstoy, *What is Art?*

AlphaBetaBestiario - Antonello Borra
Animals have always understood that mankind is not fully at home in the world. Bestiaries, hoping to teach, send out warnings. This one, of course, aims at doing the same.

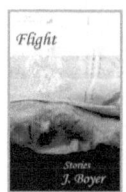

Flight and Other Stories - Jay Boyer
In *Flight and Other Stories,* we're with the fattest woman on earth as she draws her last breaths and her soul ascends toward its final reward. We meet a divorcee who can fly for no more effort than flapping her arms. We follow a middle-aged butler whose love affair with a young woman leads him first to the mysteries of bondage, and then to the pleasures of malice. Story by story, we set foot into worlds so strange as to seem all but surreal, yet everything feels familiar, each moment rings true. And that's when we recognize we're in the hands of one of America's truly original talents.

Improvisational Arguments - Anna Faktorovich
Improvisational Arguments is written in free verse to capture the essence of modern problems and triumphs. The poems clearly relate short, frequently humorous and occasionally tragic, stories about travels to exotic and unusual places, fantastic realms, abnormal jobs, artistic innovations, political objections, and misadventures with love.

Loisaida - Dan Chodorokoff
Catherine, a young anarchist estranged from her parents and squatting in an abandoned building on New York's Lower East Side is fighting with her boyfriend and conflicted about her work on an underground newspaper. After learning of a developer's plans to demolish a community garden, Catherine builds an alliance with a group of Puerto Rican community activists. Together they confront the confluence of politics, money, and real estate that rule Manhattan. All the while she learns important lessons from her great-grandmother's life in the Yiddish anarchist movement that flourished on the Lower East Side at the turn of the century. In this coming of age story, family saga, and tale of urban politics, Dan Chodorkoff explores the "principle of hope", and examines how memory and imagination inform social change.

Fomite
Burlington, Vermont

Still Time - Michael Cocchiarale

Still Time is a collection of twenty-five short and shorter stories exploring tensions that arise in a variety of contemporary relationships: a young boy must deal with the wrath of his out-of-work father; a woman runs into a man twenty years after an awkward sexual encounter; a wife, unable to conceive, imagines her own murder, as well as the reaction of her emotionally distant husband; a soon-to-be tenured English professor tries to come to terms with her husband's shocking return to the religion of his youth; an assembly line worker, married for thirty years, discovers the surprising secret life of his recently hospitalized wife. Whether a few hundred or a few thousand words, these and other stories in the collection depict characters at moments of deep crisis. Some feel powerless, overwhelmed—unable to do much to change the course of their lives. Others rise to the occasion and, for better or for worse, say or do the thing that might transform them for good. Even in stories with the most troubling of endings, there remains the possibility of redemption. For each of the characters, there is still time.

Loosestrife - Greg Delanty

This book is a chronicle of complicity in our modern lives, a witnessing of war and the destruction of our planet. It is also an attempt to adjust the more destructive blueprint myths of our society. Often our cultural memory tells us to keep quiet about the aspects that are most challenging to our ethics, to forget the violations we feel and tremors that keep us distant and numb.

Carts and Other Stories - Zdravka Evtimova

Roots and wings are the key words that best describe the short story collection, *Carts and Other Stories*, by Zdravka Evtimova. The book is emotionally multilayered and memorable because of its internal power, vitality and ability to touch both the heart and your mind. Within its pages, the reader discovers new perspectives true wealth, and learns to see the world with different eyes. The collection lives on the borders of different cultures. *Carts and Other Stories* will take the reader to wild and powerful Bulgarian mountains, to silver rains in Brussels, to German quiet winter streets and to wind bitten crags in Afghanistan. This book lives for those seeking to discover the beauty of the world around them, and will have them appreciating what they have— and perhaps what they have lost as well.

The Listener Aspires to the Condition of Music - Barry Goldensohn

"I know of no other selected poems that selects on one theme, but this one does, charting Goldensohn's career-long attraction to music's performance, consolations and its august, thrilling, scary and clownish charms. Does all art aspire to the condition of music as Pater claimed, exhaling in a swoon toward that one class act? Goldensohn is more aware than the late 19th century of the overtones of such breathing: his poems thoroughly round out those overtones in a poet's lifetime of listening."
John Peck, poet, editor, Fellow of the American Academy of Rome

Fomite
Burlington, Vermont

The Co-Conspirator's Tale - Ron Jacobs

There's a place where love and mistrust are never at peace; where duplicity and deceit are the universal currency. *The Co-Conspirator's Tale* takes place within this nebulous firmament. There are crimes committed by the police in the name of the law. Excess in the name of revolution. The combination leaves death in its wake and the survivors struggling to find justice in a San Francisco Bay Area noir by the author of the underground classic *The Way the Wind Blew: A History of the Weather Underground* and the novel *Short Order Frame Up*.

When You Remember Deir Yassin - R.L Green

When You Remember Deir Yassin is a collection of poems by R. L. Green, an American Jewish writer, on the subject of the occupation and destruction of Palestine. Green comments: "Outspoken Jewish critics of Israeli crimes against humanity have, strangely, been called 'anti-Semitic' as well as the hilariously illogical epithet 'self-hating Jews.' As a Jewish critic of the Israeli government, I have come to accept these accusations as a stamp of approval and a badge of honor, signifying my own fealty to a central element of Jewish identity and ethics: one must be a lover of truth and a friend to the oppressed, and stand with the victims of tyranny, not with the tyrants, despite tribal loyalty or self-advancement. These poems were written as expressions of outrage, and of grief, and to encourage my sisters and brothers of every cultural or national grouping to speak out against injustice, to try to save Palestine, and in so doing, to reclaim for myself my own place as part of the Jewish people." Poems in the original English are accompanied by Arabic and Hebrew translations.

Roadworthy Creature, Roadworthy Craft - Kate Magill

Words fail but the voice struggles on. The culmination of a decade's worth of performance poetry, *Roadworthy Creature, Roadworthy Craft* is Kate Magill's first full-length publication. In lines that are sinewy yet delicate, Magill's poems explore the terrain where idea and action meet, where bodies and words commingle to form a strange new flesh, a breathing text, an "I" that spirals outward from itself.

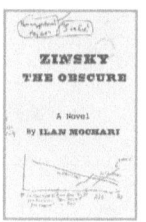

Zinsky the Obscure - Ilan Mochari

"If your childhood is brutal, your adulthood becomes a daily attempt to recover: a quest for ecstasy and stability in recompense for their early absence." So states the 30-year-old Ariel Zinsky, whose bachelor-like lifestyle belies the torturous youth he is still coming to grips with. As a boy, he struggles with the beatings themselves; as a grownup, he struggles with the world's indifference to them. *Zinsky the Obscure* is his life story, a humorous chronicle of his search for a redemptive ecstasy through sex, an entrepreneurial sports obsession, and finally, the cathartic exercise of writing it all down. Fervently recounting both the comic delights and the frightening horrors of a life in which he feels – always – that he is not like all the rest, Zinsky survives the worst and relishes the best with idiosyncratic style, as his heartbreak turns into self-awareness and his suicidal ideation into self-regard. A vivid evocation of the all-consuming nature of lust and ambition – and the forces that drive them.

Fomite
Burlington, Vermont

Love's Labours - Jack Pulaski
In the four stories and two novellas that comprise *Love's Labors* the protagonists Ben and Laura, discover in their fervid romance and long marriage their interlocking fates, and the histories that preceded their births. They also learned something of the paradox between love and all the things it brings to its beneficiaries: bliss, disaster, duty, tragedy, comedy, the grotesque, and tenderness.

Ben and Laura's story is also the particularly American tale of immigration to a new world. Laura's story begins in Puerto Rico, and Ben's lineage is Russian-Jewish. They meet in City College of New York, a place at least analogous to a melting pot. Laura struggles to rescue her brother from gang life and heroin. She is mother to her younger sister; their mother Consuelo is the financial mainstay of the family and consumed by work. Despite filial obligations, Laura aspires to be a serious painter. Ben writes, cares for and is caught up in the misadventures and surreal stories of his younger schizophrenic brother. Laura is also a story teller as powerful and enchanting as Scheherazade.

Ben struggles to survive such riches, and he and Laura endure.

TAs It Is On Earth - Peter M. Wheelwright
Four centuries after the Reformation Pilgrims sailed up the down-flowing watersheds of New England, Taylor Thatcher, irreverent scion of a fallen family of Maine Puritans, is still caught in the turbulence.

In his errant attempts to escape from history, the young college professor is further unsettled by his growing attraction to Israeli student Miryam Bluehm as he is swept by Time through the "family thing" – from the tangled genetic and religious history of his New England parents to the redemptive birthday secret of Esther Fleur Noire Bishop, the Cajun-Passamaquoddy woman who raised him and his younger half-cousin/half-brother, Bingham.

The landscapes, rivers, and tidal estuaries of Old New England and the Mayan Yucatan are also casualties of history in Thatcher's story of Deep Time and re-discovery of family on Columbus Day at a high-stakes gambling casino, rising in resurrection over the starlit bones of a once-vanquished Pequot Indian Tribe.

Kasper Planet: Comix and Tragix - Peter Schumann
The British call him Punch, the Italians, Pulchinello, the Russians, Petruchka, the Native Americans, Coyote. These are the figures we may know. But every culture that worships authority will breed a Punch-like, anti-authoritan resister. Yin and yang -- it has to happen. The Germans call him Kasper. Truth-telling and serious pranking are dangerous professions when going up against power. Bradley Manning sits naked in solitary; Julian Assange is pursued by Interpol, Obama's Department of Justice, and Amazon.com. But -- in contrast to merely human faces -- masks and theater can often slip through the bars. Consider our American Kaspers: Charlie Chaplin, Woody Guthrie, Abby Hoffman, the Yes Men -- theater people all, utilizing various forms to seed critique. Their profiles and tactics have evolved along with those of their enemies. Who are the bad guys that call forth the Kaspers? Over the last half century, with his Bread & Puppet Theater, Peter Schumann has been tireless in naming them, excoriating them with Kasperdom....
from Marc Estrin's Foreword to Planet Kasper

Fomite
Burlington, Vermont

Views Cost Extra - L.E. Smith

Views that inspire, that calm, or that terrify – all come at some cost to the viewer. In *Views Cost Extra* you will find a New Jersey high school preppy who wants to inhabit the "perfect" cowboy movie, a rural mailman disgusted with the residents of his town who wants to live with the penguins, an ailing screen writer who strikes a deal with Johnny Cash to reverse an old man's failures, an old man who ponders a young man's suicide attempt, a one-armed blind blues singer who wants to reunite with the car that took her arm on the assembly line -- and more. These stories suggest that we must pay something to live even ordinary lives.

The Empty Notebook Interrogates Itself
- Susan Thomas

The Empty Notebook began its life as a very literal metaphor for a few weeks of what the poet thought was writer's block, but was really the struggle of an eccentric persona to take over her working life. It won. And for the next three years everything she wrote came to her in the voice of the Empty Notebook, who, as the notebook began to fill itself, became rather opinionated, changed gender, alternately acted as bully and victim, had many bizarre adventures in exotic locales and developed a somewhat politically-incorrect attitude. It then began to steal the voices and forms of other poets and tried to immortalize itself in various poetry reviews. It is now thrilled to collect itself in one slim volume.

My God, What Have We Done? - Susan Weiss

In a world afflicted with war, toxicity, and hunger, does what we do in our private lives really matter? Fifty years after the creation of the atomic bomb at Los Alamos, newlyweds Pauline and Clifford visit that once-secret city on their honeymoon, compelled by Pauline's fascination with Oppenheimer, the soulful scientist. The two stories emerging from this visit reverberate back and forth between the loneliness of a new mother at home in Boston and the isolation of an entire community dedicated to the development of the bomb. While Pauline struggles with unforeseen challenges of family life, Oppenheimer and his crew reckon with forces beyond all imagining.

Finally the years of frantic research on the bomb culminate in a stunning test explosion that echoes a rupture in the couple's marriage. Against the backdrop of a civilization that's out of control, Pauline begins to understand the complex, potentially explosive physics of personal relationships.

At once funny and dead serious, *My God, What Have We Done?* sifts through the ruins left by the bomb in search of a more worthy human achievement.

The Derivation of Cowboys & Indians
- Joseph D. Reich

The Derivation of Cowboys & Indians represents a profound journey, a breakdown of The American Dream from a social, cultural, historical, and spiritual point of view. Reich examines in concise!detail the loss of the collective unconscious, commenting on our!contemporary postmodern culture with its self-interested excesses, on where and how things all go wrong, and how social/political practice rarely meets its original proclamations and promises. Reich's surreal and self-effacing satire brings this troubling message home. *The Derivations of Cowboys & Indians* is a desperate search and struggle for America's literal, symbolic, and spiritual home.

www.ingramcontent.com/pod-product-compliance
Lightning Source LLC
Chambersburg PA
CBHW060343080526
44584CB00013B/901